Getting Divorced in

New Jersey

by Jef Henninger, Esq.

Introduction
page i

Chapter 1 Deciding to File for Divorce
page 1

Chapter 2 Divorce Mediation (better than hiring a lawyer?)
page 5

Chapter 3 Hire a Lawyer or Go it Alone?
page 11

Chapter 4 Finding the Right Attorney
page 15

Chapter 5 Divorce Cost and Billing Practices
page 21

Chapter 6 The Initial Pleadings
page 25

Chapter 7 Discovery
page 29

Chapter 8 Pendente Lite Motions
page 43

Chapter 9 Parent Education Class
page 45

Chapter 10 The Case Management Conference
page 47

Chapter 11   Custody/Parenting Time Mediation
page 49

Chapter 12   The Four Way Conference
page 53

Chapter 13   Early Settlement Panel
page 57

Chapter 14   Economic Mediation
page 63

Chapter 15   Intensive Settlement Conference
page 67

Chapter 16   The Property Settlement Agreement
page 71

Chapter 17   The Uncontested Hearing
page 75

Chapter 18   Trial
page 77

Chapter 19   Post Judgment
page 85

Chapter 20   The Appeal Process
page 89

Chapter 21   DCPP Cases
page 93

Chapter 22   Domestic Violence
page 97

Introduction

I wrote this book because so many people are lost when it comes to the divorce process in New Jersey. In my opinion, an educated client is a better client. Instead of focusing on issues like equitable distribution, custody, child support and alimony, I wanted to focus on procedure. While it is possible to talk about these concepts in general terms, these concepts are too complex and ever changing to talk about with any specificity. Furthermore, most of these issues are very fact sensitive. Thus, a book focused solely on general concepts may not be that helpful to you. Instead, these issues can and should be discussed with your lawyer.

Please also keep in mind that nothing in this book should be considered legal advice and you should always defer to the court and/or your lawyer when making any decision in your case. The contents of this book are just the opinion of one lawyer. Others may disagree. Speaking of lawyers, the lawyer and attorney mean the same thing.

While I may discuss my style or my cases in this book, it is not meant to be a sales pitch for myself or my firm. While we would be happy to represent you, I am not the right lawyer for everyone, just like not everyone is the right client for my firm. We don't take every case that walks through our door. A lawyer-client relationship is a relationship like any other. What works for some will not work for others. Thus, feel free to use this book no matter who you choose to represent you.

Please note that this book is not a profit making venture; I would have to sell a ton of books to even break even for the time I spent writing this. Thankfully, my firm is very busy and I always have something to do. However, not everything lawyers do is a profit making venture. My goal is to make the client experience better regardless of whether or not this firm represents you. It is my belief that if you have a better understanding of the process, you will be able to make better decisions. This could save you time, money, energy and aggravation.

Finally, please keep in mind that I have a very unique perspective on the practice of law. I am one of the few lawyers to practice in every single county court in New Jersey. I am rather unconventional and as a result, I tend to go against the grain. Many lawyers have the same way of doing things where I have charted my own course. I'm not saying that one is better than the other, just that my approach to divorce may be different from that of your lawyer. Thus, there may be parts of this book that other lawyers would disagree with and that's fine. Everyone has their own opinion and one of the best aspects of practicing law is debating any number of issues with litigants, colleagues, judges and others.

I sincerely hope that you enjoy this book. Do not hesitate to reach out to me with any comments, suggestions or questions.

Chapter 1

Deciding to File for Divorce

Deciding to file for divorce is not easy for most. In fact, it may be the toughest decision you ever make. A divorce lawyer cannot tell you whether or not you should end your marriage. That is something you need to decide either on your own or with the assistance of others such as therapists, friends and family members. However, if you have truly decided that your marriage is in fact over, then I almost always suggest that my clients file for divorce.

The reason for this is because in New Jersey, filing for divorce essentially freezes time. For most issues, we will look at the date of filing as a critical date. For example, if we are calculating alimony, we will generally start from the date of the marriage to the date of the filing. While that may not benefit you if you may receive alimony, there are other issues where not filing could hurt you.

Let's say that you file for divorce and then a week later, your spouse cleans out a bank account and spends the money on expensive clothes and jewelry. You will have a much better claim to argue that the money your spouse took should be added back into the pot when dividing up assets. Another way to look at it is that your spouse took an advance on equitable distribution. Thus, if we are dividing up $200,000 so that you each get $100,000, whatever money your spouse spent would be deducted from his or her $100,000.

If you did not file for divorce and your spouse still spent all that money, you may be out of luck because almost all expenditures and debts during the marriage are subject to equitable distribution. Of course, there are exceptions to everything so this doesn't mean that you should go out on a shopping spree before you file for divorce. You can force your spouse to assume all of that debt, but it will just be more difficult and you may not succeed.

One of the most important concepts of divorce in New Jersey is keeping the status quo. Just because you are getting divorced does not mean that you can cancel the car insurance, move out of the house, take the kids to live somewhere else or really change anything unless you have the consent of your spouse. Thus, if you have made the decision to end your marriage, talk to a divorce lawyer before you do anything.

As I indicated before, filing for divorce does not mean that you will in fact get divorced. Your divorce is not final until a judge signs off on it. You can withdraw the divorce complaint at any time. While it is not common, I would say that at least five percent of my cases end in the parties reconciling. Some of this is shocking because the parties spent a fortune fighting each other for months. In the end, my goal is to make my clients happy, so if reconciling and dismissing the divorce makes them happy, then so be it.

Since filing for divorce doesn't mean that you will get divorced, one way of moving forward is to file for divorce and then wait some time to serve your spouse. This allows you to lock in that critical filing date without upsetting your spouse since s/he won't know that you filed. Keep in mind, however, that this will not buy you years. At best, you'll have a few months to decide what to do. If after a few weeks or months you decide not to move forward with the divorce, your lawyer will file a request for the complaint to be dismissed. The entire process should cost you less than a thousand dollars including filing fees. That's a pretty good deal to lock in some safety.

Chapter 2

Divorce Mediation

(Better than hiring a lawyer?)

As a mediator and a divorce lawyer, I feel that I can objectively weigh in on this issue. There are a number of divorce mediation concepts, but for the purposes of this discussion, divorce mediation refers to hiring a mediator to help settle the case in lieu of or before seeking the services of a lawyer. In order to discuss the pros and cons of divorce mediation, you need to understand how it works.

A divorce mediator can be a lawyer, an accountant or anyone else. I view divorce as a legal issue with emotional interference rather than an emotional issue inside the legal system. Thus, going to any mediator who is not a lawyer troubles me. This is not because I am concerned about losing business or because I am sticking up for other lawyers. Anyone who knows my business model can clearly see that this isn't true. Instead, I just don't see how a non-lawyer can possibly handle all of the complex legal issues that can arise during a divorce.

Regardless of whom you choose, your divorce mediator will be selected and retained by both of you. Therefore, the mediator will not owe a duty to either one of you. Every mediator has his or her own style. but in general the first meeting will be used to discuss and agree upon the mediation process. The mediator should ask both of you a number of questions in order to ascertain all of the issues that must be dealt with. Remember, you are not experts so you are not in a position to tell the mediator what all of the issues are. Of course, you can advise as to the issues that are important to you.

Once everyone understands the process and issues, you may be given some homework for the next session. In order to properly settle the case, the mediator needs to obtain a number of documents. Again, the exact documents required will vary based upon the mediator's style and the issues in the case. However, some examples may include credit card statements, mortgage statements, bank statements, and tax returns. The mediator may also give you documents to fill out. One of these documents may be a Case Information Statement or CIS. See the chapter on that topic for more information.

Once the mediator has reviewed this documentation, it is time to start going through the issues. The easiest issues to get out of the way are those on which you and your spouse already agree. From there, it's up to the mediator to determine how to handle the rest of the issues. The parties may dictate the order or the mediator can help to save hotly contested issues for another session so that progress can be made on others.

Regardless of how it works out, the hope is that the mediation is successful. A successful mediation results in a document that summarizes the settlement between the two of you. This entire process sounds great, but there are still countless divorce lawyers in New Jersey, and most I know are busy. This alone should tell you that there is something seriously wrong with the mediation process.

First, mediation is sold to people as the only alternative to an expensive divorce. This couldn't be farther from the truth. There is no guarantee that mediation will be successful or that it will even be cheaper than hiring a lawyer. Divorce is what you make of it, and if you hire the wrong lawyer, you will make your divorce expensive. If you and your spouse are on such good terms that you can agree on a mediator, you can probably sit down with your respective lawyers and hammer out a settlement a lot quicker and for the same amount of money.

The second issue with mediation is that your spouse may be able to wiggle out of the agreement once s/he speaks to a lawyer. Thus, all of that time and money you spent getting to that agreement may be wasted if the settlement is worth nothing to you in the end.

Yet another issue is that the mediator is not your lawyer. Thus, he or she cannot give legal advice to either one of you. As a result, you may lose out on a number of issues that you could have used to your advantage. There is a huge difference between taking your spouse to the cleaners and getting what is fair. Sometimes getting what is fair involves at least a discussion about what is to your advantage so that you know what to ask for and how to structure your negotiation strategy.

Since the mediator is not your lawyer, he or she cannot represent either one of you. Thus, when you do settle your case, you either have to file for divorce on your own or hire a lawyer. If you don't hire a lawyer, you will be forced to navigate the court system on your own and could experience further delay. In contrast, a divorce lawyer can help you get a quick court date.

Some people pushing divorce mediation also hide the fact that there could be up to three court-ordered divorce mediation sessions in your divorce case. Too many people think that if they don't select divorce mediation, they will have to spend a fortune and go to trial. As will be detailed later in this book, there are a number of options, most through the courts, such as four-way conferences, parenting-time mediation, early settlement panel, economic mediation and intensive settlement conference. Want even better news? Some of these programs are either completely free or partially free. In addition to these court programs, both parties can hire a mediator at any time on their own to help them mediate the case with the assistance of their respective lawyers.

Of course, divorce mediation does work for some people. In my opinion, however, these cases are the clear minority. What most people don't realize is that if their divorce case is not handled properly, they could be stuck in court for years trying to deal with or fix the issues caused by their quick and cheap divorce. When getting divorced, doing it the right way can help you get piece of mind and save you time, money and aggravation in the future.

I've seen too many people pay a fortune to litigate post-judgment motions because they were penny-wise and pound-foolish in their divorce case. Don't make any assumptions. If you are considering divorce mediation, discuss this issue with a lawyer that can represent you in the divorce or do the mediation. For most cases that are suitable for mediation, I would likely make less money representing either party in the divorce itself. Nevertheless, more often than not I recommend that both sides get a lawyer rather than pursue mediation.

If you are going to select mediation instead of hiring a divorce lawyer, do so with the above information in mind. Don't assume that it will be cheaper or easier. Don't assume that it is the only alternative to an all-out expensive war that will bankrupt the two of you. Do it because you think it is the best thing to do.

Chapter 3

Hire a Lawyer or Go it Alone?

To me, this is a question that shouldn't even be considered. While almost everyone going through a divorce hires a lawyer, there are some people that decide that they can handle the process on their own. I'm not one for quotes but the best quote ever is "a person who represents himself has a fool for a client." Another way to look at it is, if you wouldn't do surgery on yourself, why would you be your own lawyer?

There are several reasons why people try to go it alone, but the most common one is money. There are two very common scenarios: (1) the couple doesn't have much money and thus, there is nothing to fight over; or (2) one spouse is keeping all the money from the other.

Just because you think you have nothing to fight over

doesn't mean that this is true. However, even if that is the case, hiring a lawyer shouldn't be that expensive. Your lawyer will indeed confirm that there is nothing to fight over and then draft up the correct settlement agreement to protect you. You'd be surprised how many people have hidden debts and other liabilities that can come back to haunt the other spouse after the divorce. Paying a little bit of money to avoid this seems like a great insurance policy.

While it is true that many lawyers seem to charge $5000 for every single divorce case, there are some (such as my firm) that charge based upon the complexity of the case. If it really is a "nothing divorce" as we sometimes call it, then it could cost you as little as $1,000 in legal fees!

If the other side is keeping all the money from you or you has assets that are otherwise not accessible, you may still be able to hire a lawyer. Your lawyer can file a motion to force the other spouse to advance counsel fees to you so that you can pay your lawyer. This application is granted so often that most lawyers will not even force the other lawyer to file the motion. If the assets are not accessible, your lawyer can get paid at the end of the case when the assets are liquidated and divided up.

If you are truly indigent, and by that I mean not working and on some type of government assistance and there are no assets, you can try to apply for legal services. However, the legal services budget has been slashed in the last few years and they may not be able to help you. Of course, it doesn't hurt to make a call but don't be surprised if you get turned down.

Despite all of these warnings, if you are going to go it alone or go *"pro se"* as it is known, do not pay for any documents! We've all seen the billboards: Divorce $399! These "divorce mills" as I call them are simply selling you a packet of papers that you can get for free from the court, legal services or the library. It kills me that people are being taken advantage of like this. Again, if your divorce was that easy, you could have hired a real lawyer for just a little more money. I'm hoping I live to see the day when these divorce mills go out of business.

Chapter 4

Finding the Right Attorney

There is no easy answer here. Hiring a lawyer is just like establishing any other relationship. Not everyone is going to click. Selecting the right lawyer is a bit of a crap shoot for the most part since it is so hard to tell who is going to do a good job for you and if you will click with that person. The easiest thing to do is to tell you how not to pick a lawyer.

You should not base your selection of lawyer on any of these criteria: age, race, gender, religion, location of office, how nice the office looks and hourly rate. Some of that may sound obvious but too many people want a lawyer from one religion or another, a man or a woman, or a lawyer of one race or another. This is nonsense, plain and simple.

Office location, size and appearance shouldn't play a part either. Some people want a lawyer who has an office right next to the court house. Anyone can sign a lease. You don't need any real qualifications. Others want someone in that county while some want one from out of county. The in county thing makes no sense but the way it has been explained to me is that if you are from that county, the judges will like you better. Do you really have such little faith in our justice system that you think it is that corrupt? Sadly, some lawyers actually think that and they think I am insane for having such a wide practice area. Judges apply the law to the facts without regard to who the lawyer is or where s/he is from. It's that simple.

There is some validity to hiring a lawyer out of county. In smaller counties, the family court lawyers are a very tight network. Many of them hang out with each other on a regular basis. The concern is that hiring another local lawyer may be detrimental to the case since s/he will put his/her relationship with the other lawyer over the interests of the client. I've seen this happen, but to say that all lawyers in that county are like that is painting with too broad of a brush. If this is your real concern, ask some questions when you are talking to the lawyer you want to hire. Just don't rule out every lawyer in that county automatically.

Office appearance is nonsense as well. Anyone with half a practice can pay an exorbitant rent for a fancy office. This does not mean that s/he is a good lawyer. In fact, s/he may be over compensating for some other areas that are lacking. I have some nice offices. I have some others that are modest. Either way, I paid for great locations but got great value. The less I have to pay in rent, the less I have to charge my clients.

I love hearing that clients need to hire a "shark" or a "bulldog." Trust me, you don't need either. Divorce is mostly about working together towards a compromise. Of course, there are times when the lawyers have to fight it out but there is a way to do that and a way not to do that. Thus, you need someone who can pivot. When it's time to negotiate in a diplomatic fashion, then that's what should happen. When it's time to slug it out, then the lawyer needs to pivot to slug it out with the best of them. Attorneys that have a reputation for being bulldogs or sharks are more commonly known as jerks that no one wants to deal with. We all know who they are. It's amazing how people that want to waste their money making divorce more complicated than it really has to be somehow find these people.

You also should not choose a lawyer based upon hourly rate, except that you should be wary of rates that are too high or too low. Hourly rates for a good divorce lawyer range from $300 to $450 an hour in my opinion. Some lawyers may have associates with hourly rates lower than $300, and that is fine. However, the primary lawyer in the firm should not be below $300. Of course, there are some great lawyers that have such low hourly rates, but I would be very cautious. Think of it this way, if this lawyer was so amazing, why would he be charging so little? How could these other lawyers stay in business? Less educated people pick a lawyer based upon price and as a result, they may have a lower end clientele. Your lawyer should not be desperate for business.

Low hourly rates may also be deceptive. Just because one lawyer's rate is lower than another's does not mean your case will be less expensive. Some lawyers lure you with a low hourly rate but then double the amount of work that needs to be done. As a result, you wind up paying more than if you went with the lawyer with the higher hourly rate. My firm is not the cheapest but we are focused on client satisfaction because we want our clients to refer their friends and family to us. That is not going to happen if they feel like we ripped them off. Thus, we are very careful with our billing practices so that our clients get the best result for the best price. Is your lawyer doing that?

Likewise, finding a lawyer who has a rate of $500 an hour or above is silly. There reaches a point where you are not really getting much if anything at all for such a price besides a huge bill. Absent the most complicated, big money cases, these lawyers are not necessary. And unless you have a martial estate worth $10 million, your case is not that complicated. Even then, lawyers with lower hourly rates can probably get the job done just as well.

Another issue to consider is choosing a solo lawyer, a mid-size firm or a large firm. Some lawyers don't want to create an empire. They just want to practice law in a small area. I have a mid-size firm because we handle the entire state and I need to space out the work. However, we are still a boutique firm in that we only practice a limited amount of areas. Thus, our size is indicative of our popularity. Big firms, however, are a completely different animal. They do everything and they are big for a reason. In other words, big firms can mean big bills. Of course, there are exceptions. I have worked on cases with one of the top lawyers from a big firm and we worked well together to settle the case. However, I have seen too many other cases cost ten times more than what they should have. Thus, don't assume that hiring a big firm will really get you anywhere in your divorce case. Instead, hire a big firm because you like the lawyer that works there and you would hire him/her if s/he worked at a much smaller firm.

The internet has become the go-to place for researching lawyers. Unfortunately, too many clients get wowed by fancy, expensive websites. Before you get bowled over, ask yourself who wrote the website. Look at the very bottom of the site. Chances are, you will see something like "designed by X company" or just a reference to another company's name. Most firms hire expensive companies to write their content and get them to the top of Google. The most popular one is Findlaw, but there are others. Thus, that content you like is written by someone that might not even be in New Jersey and is almost certainly not a lawyer. All of our content is written by either myself or one of my employees. If I don't write it, I at least edit it and read over it. Thus, you can be sure that whatever you read is our voice. That's the entire purpose of our websites and blogs: not to rank on Google but to give you the potential client insight into how we think.

Chapter 5

Divorce Cost and Billing Practices

In New Jersey, a lawyer cannot charge a flat fee for a family court case such as divorce. However, there are still a few unscrupulous lawyers who attempt to get away with it. You should avoid them at all cost. A law-abiding lawyer will charge you a retainer, which is an upfront payment that is deposited into a trust account. A trust account is a type of escrow account. If and when the lawyer earns that money, it is transferred into the business account. Any money in the trust account at the end of the case is refunded back to the client. Thus, all divorce retainers are refundable unless and until they are used up.

As previously mentioned, each lawyer has an hourly rate. The hourly rate should cover all work done on the file. This includes phone calls, which tends to upset some clients that do not understand that the only thing a lawyer has to sell is time. Instead of billing exact minutes, lawyers bill in tenths of an hour or quarter hours. Thus, if you speak to a lawyer on the phone for 3 minutes, it is billed against the retainer as 6 minutes or 15 minutes depending on the billing practice of that lawyer. We bill in tenths of an hour. While there is no written rule, I don't bill for every single phone call, although I am permitted to do so. If it is very quick and with very little substance, I won't bill for it.

All of this time gets billed and put on an invoice. Attorneys that are not stuck in last century use a computerized billing system while some others use time sheets. Regardless, at some point the lawyer generates an itemized invoice which is presented to the client. This invoice shows the client everything that was done on the file. It could be generated monthly or at some other interval. If the retainer has been exceeded, the lawyer will likely ask for more money. However, if the client has no money but has an asset such as a house that can be liquidated, the lawyer may wait for the end of the case to get paid in full.

A matrimonial lawyer cannot set a contingency fee. That is, the lawyer cannot set his or her fee based upon whether the case is won or lost. That is only permitted in certain cases outside of family law such as personal injury. Since most divorces are settled, you can see why this would never really work.

How the lawyer gets paid and how much varies. For some reason, many lawyers in New Jersey have settled on $5,000 as a magic number for the average divorce case. We start most of our cases off at $2,500 or less for easier cases. We accept credit cards while others do not. Depending on the case, we may also be able to accept a payment plan while others do not. If your spouse is keeping you from all of the money, your lawyer may be able to file a motion with the court to force your spouse to advance you money for your lawyer's fees.

The final cost of your case depends on a variety of factors. One of the most important factors is the lawyer you select and his or her style on billing. As previously mentioned, we work hard to get our clients a great result for a great price. As a result, our fees are often lower than our adversaries. We know this through a variety of sources, but one of them is when the other side files a motion and asks for counsel fees. They have to disclose how much their client paid them and how much they have charged their client.

Of course, another important factor is you. How often will you call your lawyer? I've had clients call me several times a day every single day even though they knew it was costing them money. The average person doesn't do this, so his/her bills are much lower. The cost also depends on what you are fighting over. The cost to fight over something must be weighed against the value of that item. For example, I once had a client try to pay me $5,000 to fight over $500. I told him that he was crazy and that I wouldn't do it. Almost a decade later we've become friends and he has referred several cases to me. He is very thankful that I didn't rip him off. If your lawyer doesn't discuss the costs of fighting the case, ask how much it will cost and whether it is worth the fight.

Thus, there is no straight answer. In our office, the majority of our cases cost our clients between $1,500 on the low end to $10,000 on the higher end. Of course, there are cases that exceed $10,000 but on average, most of ours don't.

Chapter 6

The Initial Pleadings

Now that you have decided to file for divorce and you have your lawyer signed up, it's time to file the divorce complaint. Pulling the trigger gives more people anxiety than any other issue in divorce court. As scary as the divorce complaint may seem, you must realize that it's a rather simple document that is only confusing because it hasn't been updated for today's world.

In order to get divorced, you have to prove a cause of action. Prior to 2007, you had to allege and prove one of these causes of action: adultery, desertion, extreme physical or mental cruelty, living separately for 18 months, addiction to drugs or alcohol for one year, institutionalization in a mental hospital for 2 years, imprisonment for 18 months or deviant sexual conduct.

Most people opted to choose extreme mental cruelty but that led most to fudge the facts that led to the breakdown of the marriage. However, New Jersey now has irreconcilable differences, which probably accounts for over 90% of the causes of action in divorce cases.

With irreconcilable differences, neither side has to move out and you don't have to even explain why you want the divorce, let alone make a number of allegations against your spouse. There is almost no reason to use the other causes of action, and New Jersey should have done away with them in my opinion.

In a perfect world, a divorce complaint would be a very simple fill-in-the-blank document. I think it is purposely left confusing so that people don't get the idea to do it on their own. Of course, this has led people to seek out divorce mills that sell them a packet of paper for $399 when they could get the same information for free elsewhere.

Now that I'm off my soapbox, once the divorce complaint and companion documents are filled out, they are filed with the court along with the appropriate filing fee. After about a week or so, the complaint is returned with a docket number on it. A docket number is the court's way to keep track of the file, and each complaint gets its own docket number.

Notice how the complaint only went to the court? Your spouse needs to be served. If you don't serve your spouse within about 3 to 6 months, the court will automatically dismiss your complaint. To serve your spouse, your lawyer will draft a document called a summons that is affixed to the front of the complaint. This will then be served upon your spouse.

You can serve your spouse through any method. The old method was to use the sheriff's office, but I have rarely used this approach. Certified mail works well for most cases while a process server can be used for others. Many people filing for divorce are scared about what will happen when their spouse is served but in almost all of my cases, there hasn't been a negative reaction. This is thanks in part to the irreconcilable differences cause of action since your spouse is not getting a document filled with allegations about all the bad things s/he has done to you.

Within 35 days of being served, your spouse needs to file a responsive pleading such an appearance, answer or answer and counterclaim. Again, our system could be simplified here. Most lawyers choose to file and Answer and Counterclaim. This is one document in two parts. The Answer responds to the allegations in the complaint, usually through a denial. The Counterclaim part then says that your spouse also wants to divorce you. Thus, he or she will usually mirror what you put into your complaint.

Again, this might seem silly in that you are on one hand denying the allegations or at least failing to admit them but then you are making the same allegations. By allegations, I mean the paragraphs in your divorce complaint which really don't seem like allegations anyway. Your spouse really can't stop you from getting divorced so litigants would be served if this form were simplified. The purpose in filing a counterclaim is if the person filing the complaint dismissed the case or otherwise fails to follow through with it, the divorce case will still go on. Otherwise, if you just file an answer, the Plaintiff can dismiss at any time.

Speaking of the Plaintiff, the person that files for the complaint first is the Plaintiff and the other spouse is the Defendant. It usually doesn't matter who is the Plaintiff and who is the Defendant. I see no advantage or disadvantage other than the Answer having to pay a smaller filing fee. What is important is that whoever wants to file for divorce file right away for the reasons previously mentioned.

While it is sometimes overlooked by lawyers and courts, the Plaintiff should file an answer to the counterclaim. I hate to be a broken record, but this is really a pointless exercise that should be done away with. There is no filing fee for filing this answer. With all those initial pleadings out of the way, we can finally get down to business.

Chapter 7

Discovery

In order for your lawyer to size up your case to see what you are entitled to, you need to exchange discovery with the other side. Discovery is essentially a fact gathering process for both sides. Everything must be disclosed and nothing can remain a secret. Thus, all financial records, potential witnesses, expert reports and other information will be given to the other side. This is yet another reason why most divorce cases don't go to trial. Both sides have access to the same information. There really shouldn't be any surprises at trial.

There are a number of discovery instruments that can be used by your lawyer to gather information including the following: Case Information Statements, Interrogatories, Notice to Produce, Request for Admissions, Subpoenas and Depositions. It is important to understand each one so you can understand what your lawyer is doing or not doing and why. I am covering this topic now because I think discovery should be completed as soon as possible. Remember, the faster the case is over, the cheaper your case may be. I give my clients the following to help them speed up their cases:

-

SPEED UP YOUR DIVORCE CASE

The discovery process can really drag out a divorce case. For whatever reason, most lawyers wait months to start this process. By starting it early, it can dramatically speed up the resolution of your case. For example, it may take you weeks or even months to obtain certain documents. It would be better to find that out sooner rather than later.

While we cannot force the other side to give us their discovery requests sooner, we can give you an idea of some of the questions that you will have to answer and some of the documents that you will have to provide. Please review the documents provided which include a "notice to produce," "interrogatories" and "custody interrogatories." Custody interrogatories are only included if custody may be an issue. Please be advised that these are the same discovery requests that will be sent to your spouse.

Besides being able to respond to the other lawyer's discovery requests a lot faster than normal, providing these documents to us will also help us analyze your case much faster than we otherwise could. While the documents needed in each case may vary, the most important documents in most cases include the following: mortgage statements, all bank statements, retirement account statement (pension, IRA, 401K, etc.) and credit card statements (regardless of whose name it is in). I suggest that you provide at least the last two years of statements, but keep in mind that the other side may ask for statements dating back as much as five or more years ago. Please also keep a copy of these statements as the case progresses and provide them to us every three months unless we request otherwise.

Your CIS is the most important document in your case. If you haven't already been provided with one, one is enclosed. It will take some time to complete and I suggest you do the best job you can. If alimony may be an issue, it is important that your Schedules A, B and C be as accurate as possible. In addition to your bank and credit card statements, your utility bills will also help us substantiate those numbers. Thus, please provide us with at least one year of utility bills.

I realize that some of these items may take time to get which is why we are requesting them now. If some of these items are impossible to obtain, please provide us with specifics as to what items you cannot obtain and why.

If your lawyer is not asking for these items to be completed right away, ask why. Tell him or her that you want to speed up your case and that there is no reason to wait for the case management conference. Of course, if your lawyer gives you a really good reason to wait, consider that advice. I just can't think of any reason myself.

Case Information Statement

The Case Information Statement or CIS (not CSI as everyone seems to call it) is the backbone to your entire case. You have probably never seen anything like it before, and it could appear to be a daunting task. That's because it is! If you do it correctly, it should take you at least eight hours to complete. You should put a ton of thought into it.

A CIS covers several issues. One of them is your past and present income. We need to see how you are paid, by whom, how often and how you were paid in the recent past. Your lawyer will be looking for issues such as self employment, changes in income, fluctuations in income, overtime and other issues. The CIS will ask for proof to support your claims, so be sure that they are accurate.

The CIS will also ask you for a household budget. It looks first at all money coming in and then at all money going out. The CIS asks for monthly figures even though some items are infrequent or even once a year. In these situations, your lawyer will likely advise you to add up the yearly expenses and divide by 12.

The CIS also asks for the family budget and your current budget. If there is no separation, your lawyer may ask you to only fill out one column and not the other. Every lawyer has her own style, so ask before you assume anything.

These first two parts of the CIS will help your lawyer and the court establish support figures, i.e. child support and alimony. If alimony is not an issues in your case, then the family budget becomes less important and you may be able to use estimates instead of hard numbers. Ask your lawyer if this is okay to do. If it is, be sure to indicate somewhere that the figures are just estimates so that you don't get in trouble later if these figures are proved wrong.

The next part of the CIS will ask you for a statement of assets and liabilities. This will help determine all of the equitable distribution issues in your case. Unless you have really complicated assets, this section should not be difficult to fill out. However, you might not have exact figures. For example, if you haven't done an appraisal, you don't know how much the house is worth but could guess or use a website for an estimate. You should have statements for all of your liabilities so estimates should be unnecessary. The sum of your liabilities is then subtracted from your total assets to determine your net worth. Hopefully it's a positive number, but far too many divorce cases have a negative number.

When filling out the liabilities portion, don't assume that you know of all debts in your name or your spouse's name. Instead, I suggest pulling a credit report from all three credit bureaus and looking it over carefully. This is free if you go to www.annualcreditreport.gov. You may discovery that you have been the victim of identity theft, that you had a credit card you forgot about, that there is a judgment against you, or that your spouse is taking out debt in your name without telling you. Provide all three reports to your lawyer, but keep a copy for your own records. You should contest any negative items as well. While the reports will not contain your credit score, you will get a better picture of your credit to see how you will move forward post-divorce.

One of the most overlooked issues in a CIS is backing up and/or explaining all of your figures. If your case is rather simple and will not be litigated heavily, you might be able to get away with taking a few shortcuts. This is a decision you can only make after discussing the entire case with your lawyer. However, if you really want to do things the right way, you will have to show your work just like you did in algebra class.

Backing up some of your numbers is easy if you have the statements that you relied upon. Again, all of your liabilities should have some type of current bill showing how much you pay each month and how much of a balance is remaining. You should have one statement for each liability appearing on your credit report even if there is a zero balance.

Backing up the figures for your assets is another story. There are websites like Zillow that you can use to estimate the value of your house. You can also use Kelly Blue Book to value your car. Regardless of the asset and how you come up with the value, you should have either a print out of what you used or an explanation of how you arrived at the value. Otherwise, a fight could erupt over how you came up with the number. Remember, the value for this purpose is the total value regardless of the liability. The true value (after subtracting the liability) will be determined later.

Showing how you came up with your figures for the family budget may be much more difficult. Your lawyer may not even want you to do this, so check with him or her first. In cases where this is important, I like to go all out and back up everything, but that's just how I practice.

One of the easiest ways to do this is to create a spreadsheet for each expense listed on the CIS. There should be 12 rows for each expense; one for each month. Put the monthly figure for each expense in each row. To find these figures, you can use monthly bills, credit card statements, bank statements and receipts. If you still have to estimate, explain why you are doing so and how you arrived at those figures. You will then total up each row using the "sum function" and divide by 12 to arrive at the monthly figure.

This is important to do not only for one-time expenses such as car registration but also for monthly expenses that change over time. Your electric bill will likely be more expensive in the summer, while your heating bill will be the opposite. If you have children in sports or other extracurricular activities, these expenses will likely be seasonal as well.

While you will now have a very accurate CIS, you still need to support your numbers. There are two ways to do this. You can attach yet another sheet explaining how you arrived at each and every figure. Or you can do it in the same spreadsheet. For example, you would just add another column explaining the source of each number. You could also attach every single document to the CIS itself but this would make your CIS huge and therefore cumbersome. All of these items should be provided in discovery anyway or are otherwise discoverable. So you will want them readily available but your lawyer will probably not want them attached to the CIS.

I know that this all seems like a ton of work, but don't you want your divorce done the right way? By calculating all of your figures correctly and showing how you got to them, you stand a better chance of your CIS being accepted as accurate by the court and third parties such as mediators and arbitrators. You may also lessen the ability of the other side to fight you on numbers. Most importantly, you will stand up better if you are ever questioned about your numbers. You won't have to remember anything! Even years later, you will know exactly how you arrived at those numbers.

Technically, your CIS should be filed within a few weeks of your initial pleading. However, this is rarely done and the court knows it. Thus, the standard case management form (more on that later) includes a section for a CIS due date. If you really want to speed up your case, you should have your CIS back to your lawyer as soon as possible. In my practice, I give out a blank CIS right away and ask for a completed copy in 30 days.

When your CIS gets back to your lawyer in 30 days, your lawyer has plenty of time to read through it and clean it up if necessary. Making your lawyer work with a tight deadline is no way to do work. A fully completed CIS also allows your lawyer to quickly size up the case and figure out where to focus his or her efforts. Within minutes of looking at a completed CIS, I can size up the entire case and figure out with pretty good accuracy what issues can be settled quickly and which ones will be contested.

Interrogatories

Interrogatories are a set of questions given to the other side of the case to elicit information. Like many things in law, we have to use big, old fashioned words. Just view these as nothing more than questions and don't be intimidated even if there are be a ton of them!

Because these interrogatories may be quite lengthy, you don't want to save them for the last minute. You will have to certify that your responses are correct so you have to make sure that everything you say is accurate. You don't want to be on the witness stand later trying to explain your way out of an answer because you didn't put a lot of thought into the question. Your lawyer should review your responses before submitting them. Some of these questions may also be subject to an objection or be irrelevant to your case. If your lawyer is just submitting whatever you wrote without any editing, you selected the wrong lawyer!

Notice to Produce

A notice to produce is a request to provide documents from the other side. Some of these documents may be easily accessible while others may be more difficult to obtain. Again, this should be started as soon as possible so that you do not run out of time if certain documents take a long time to obtain. Also, your lawyer should be reviewing the documents requested first to make sure that all of the requests were proper. You don't want to take six weeks to track down documents only to find out that you really didn't have to provide them anyway.

Request for Admissions

Requests for admissions are basically a list of yes or no answers to a number of statements. However, instead of yes or no, the answer is admit or deny. An example could be: "Do you admit or deny that Husband's parents provided $20,000 to the parties prior to purchasing the house?" A follow up could then be: "If you answered admit to the previous request, do you admit or deny that the $20,000 was a loan to the parties?"

Notice that the request was broken down into individual components. A poorly drafted request would have included both the request about the $20,000 and about it being considered a loan. If the answer was "deny," you don't know what part of the request is actually being denied. In my practice, such requests are seldom used by other lawyers, but that doesn't mean they shouldn't be used in the right cases. Such requests can be an effective method of narrowing the dispute in a case, especially when used along with the other discovery devices described in this chapter.

Subpoenas

A subpoena is a legal request for either testimony or production of documents. It has the same effect as a court order. A subpoena for testimony is a "subpoena ad testificandum," whereas a subpoena for the production of documents is a "subpoena duces tecum." Again with the old fashioned words! It would be helpful if the legal world entered the 21st century at some point in my lifetime, but I'm not going to hold my breath.

When a subpoena is properly served, the receiving party must comply with it unless it files a motion to quash. If the subpoena was not properly served, then the receiving party may not have to comply. Proper service is governed by local rules. A motion to quash is a request made to the court to dismiss the subpoena so that the receiving party does not have to comply with it. Even if the motion to quash is denied, merely filing it will delay compliance with the subpoena.

If the subpoena is for testimony, this testimony is usually for a trial or for deposition. If this was unexpected, you should discuss your response with your lawyer at this point because the case just became very serious.

Depositions

A deposition is an opportunity for a lawyer to question someone—for example the opposing party or a witness—prior to trial. This almost always happens in a lawyer's conference room. The party being deposed has the right to have a lawyer present. A court reporter will be present, and he or she will administer an oath to the witness. This oath carries with it the same weight as testifying under oath at trial. As a result, anything said must be the truth.

The purpose of a deposition is to get information. The way this is often done is by asking as many questions as possible. The lawyer wouldn't want to do this at trial so now is the time to ask anything and everything (in most cases) to nail the witness down to a story on any and all issues. As a result, depositions can take many hours. While I appreciate the lawyer's job to nail down all of these issues, most depositions go on far too long. There can only be so many contested issues in a case. Getting to the meat of the issues is important.

After the deposition, the court stenographer will mail out a transcript, which is a verbatim record of everything that was said during the deposition. Either lawyer can then use this transcript in other proceedings such as motions and trials. The deposition transcript will help the lawyer tailor the case at trial because the lawyer knows exactly who will say what. As a result, most cases will settle after depositions because the factual disputes will be limited. If the witness were to testify differently at trial, the lawyer will confront the witness with his prior sworn statements. As a result, the witness will often lose credibility with the court.

Depositions in divorce cases are rare. For one, they are expensive. You have to pay your lawyer to prepare for it, attend it, and then review the transcript afterward. This will likely take 15 or more hours. Multiply that by your lawyer's hourly rate and you can quickly see how expensive it is. In addition, you have to pay for the court stenographer. This isn't cheap either. Thus, you should have a very involved case to even think about needing a deposition.

Of course, it is possible to only depose one witness for about a half hour just to get their testimony on the record. However, I find that other discovery methods can be utilized that are more cost effective than a quick deposition, such as a private investigator.

Private Investigator

I never suggest hiring a private investigator on your own for your divorce case. If you want to find out if your spouse is cheating on you, that's a different story. However, you should first find out if this even matters to the divorce case if you think it could go that way. In New Jersey, adultery usually doesn't get you anywhere except further into debt as you pay more money to your lawyer.

A private investigator can be a great resource to interview witnesses, especially if you aren't sure if they are friendly or hostile. A private investigator can also be used to prove other issues such as if your spouse is abusing substances, taking the child around dangerous people or not really spending time with the child. Whatever the purpose is, be sure that it is relevant to an issue in your case. Remember, your emotions should not play a part here. Let your lawyer guide you.

Chapter 8

Pendente Lite Motions

Pendente Lite motions (usually pronounced pen-den-tay lee-tay although there are variations) or simply just called PL motions, is what New Jersey calls its temporary motions. A pendente lite order stays in effect until the case is over unless another order overturns it first.

Examples of PL motions include but are not limited to:

-A request that one parent be designated the custodial parent

-A request that neither party take the children out of state

-A request that the other spouse not bring the children around his/her paramour

-A request for a parenting time schedule for the non-custodial parent

-Child support

-Spousal support

-Counsel fees subject to final allocation

-Freezing a bank account so that neither party can dissipate the money

-Distributing some portion of money in an account to either or both parties subject to final allocation

A PL motion should not be taken lightly. No matter what the issue is, it will take your lawyer at least a few hours to work on it out of court, prepare for court and then argue the motion in court. Thus, if the matter can be settled out of court, it could save you thousands. In fact, the right PL motion could account for half of your total divorce bill. While this may not be common, it is possible.

While I put the chapter for PL motions here, it could happen at any time. I have filed PL motions at the same time as the divorce complaint. There could also be numerous PL motions. Hopefully, your case doesn't involve any.

Chapter 9

Parent Education Class

In all divorce cases involving minor children, except those where there is a domestic violence restraining order, you will be ordered to attend a parent education class. The fee for this class is $25 and is paid as part of your filing fee. This is why filing fees are cheaper if you are filing for divorce without children.

You will receive a court notice for the class in the mail a few weeks after the initial pleading is filed. The class will be held at the courthouse, but the good news is that your lawyer will not attend. The class is designed to teach how to handle the divorce with your children. Most clients report that it was at least somewhat, if not very, helpful and informative. You also don't have to worry about seeing your spouse. Plaintiffs will be there on one day and defendants will be there on another.

Please note that attendance is mandatory. Don't even think about skipping out on it. While I understand that taking off of work is an inconvenience, this is all part of the process. Hopefully, you will also find the class informative and that could lead to an easier case. As a result, you may not only save money but your children will be much better off in the long run.

Chapter 10

The Case Management Conference

Unless you filed an early PL motion, this should be your first real court appearance. The purpose of the case management conference is to fill out a Case Management Order. This order sets forth the responsibilities of both parties and due dates for various tasks. It may also set up the Early Settlement Panel date. Please note that in some counties, you don't actually have to go to court. Instead, the lawyers just submit an order to the court for the judge to sign. However, some judges require an appearance.

If attendance is optional, I choose to go to the Case Management Conference whenever there is something I want to run by the judge. Most judges will allow you to conference with them to get guidance on an issue that could hold up the case or help resolve it quickly. This is a great opportunity to get some insight into the case.

The Case Management Order will set forth due dates for the following items (if necessary):

-Sending out (or "propounding") discovery requests

-Responding to discovery requests

-Submitting the Case Information Statements

-Depositions

-Production of bank account balances

-Appraisal of personal property

-Valuation of pensions

-Appraisal of the martial home and other property

-Appraisal of businesses

-Export reports

The court can also order that the parties attend parenting time mediation although you may not get a date right away. If possible, some courts will also give you a date for ESP. (See subsequent chapters for parenting time mediation and ESP). However, you could be in ESP in three months or less, putting everyone under a big time crunch. As a result, I require that my clients already have the CIS done. In almost all cases, I would have already sent out discovery. Thus, my side of the case is already ahead of schedule.

Chapter 11

Custody/Parenting Time Mediation

Custody/parenting time mediation is a great way to resolve custody disputes with your spouse. The success rate is very high across New Jersey, but I am sure it varies from county to county based upon the personnel involved. The best part about this program is that it comes at no cost to you! The mediator is free and your lawyer will not be there. It doesn't get any better than that. Since anything said during the mediation is non-evidential, you can speak freely without worrying about your words being used against you later. Of course, you don't want to tip your hand to your strategy, so before you spill the beans as to your trial strategy, talk to your lawyer.

Solving your custody and parenting time issues without involving a judge and/or your lawyer will save you a ton of money. In fact, you could chop your final bill in half just by settling this issue here. Because it happens relatively early in your case, your lawyer might not have started to gear up for a big battle yet, which will save you thousands. Of course, there are some exceptions. If things are getting ugly in a hurry, you don't want your lawyer to do nothing until you see what the outcome of mediation is. In fact, some of the information gathered prior to the mediation in preparation for a big war can help you settle the case. Luckily, the majority of cases settle without having to even prepare for a war.

I rarely find a need to prepare my client for custody/parenting time mediation. However, if you are unsure as to what to ask for or if you have any other questions, it can't hurt to discuss it with your lawyer before you attend. The parenting time mediators are often very skilled and unbiased. They will walk you through the different options and hopefully get the two of you to come to some type of an agreement.

The best way to approach this is with an open mind. This is not the Jerry Springer Show. You are not there to yell at your spouse, and the mediator is not there to scold either of you. Have a goal in mind as to what you want but at the same time, be flexible. Let the other side talk no matter how much it kills you inside. Feel free to take notes so that you can properly and calmly respond to the various points the other side is making.

If you can come up with an agreement, the mediator will draft up a memorandum of understanding. That will then be forwarded to the respective lawyers so that they can sign off on it. Thus, this allows you to back out of it if you later change your mind or if your lawyer explains that you did the wrong thing. Nevertheless, it may still be good practice to not sign anything until your lawyer reviews it. Ask him or her how to handle the situation.

If custody/parenting time mediation was unproductive, you should meet with your lawyer to debrief. Your lawyer should know what went wrong; what the other side said and asked for; etc. You will then need to come up with a plan for the next steps in the case.

Chapter 12

The Four Way Conference

A four way conference is an opportunity for you and your lawyer to meet with your spouse and his/her lawyer in an effort to settle the case or at least work out some of the issues. It is completely optional. Just like a PL motion, it can happen at any time and occur more than once. However, it is not right for every case. If the case is already nasty, putting everyone in the same room can only make things worse. If the other lawyer is really difficult to deal with, there is no point in wasting your time. However, when it's right to do, a four way can pay off big time.

Since this is completely optional, there are no requirements as to when it happens, what you discuss, what you bring, etc. In fact, there may be nothing to even prepare for. After all, it's just a discussion among four people. Just like any other form of mediation, whatever happens there stays there. You have the right to talk freely, but at the same time, you don't want the other side to know your strategy, your fears, or your complete position.

As I have already said, now is not the time to think that you are on the Jerry Springer Show. Really, there is never a time for that. If your lawyer even thinks that that could happen, a four way conference is not a good idea. Like all types of mediation, you should have an open mind but don't just give in to whatever the other side wants. Instead, listen to the other side and don't get offended. Have a poker face. If you need to discuss something with your lawyer, feel free to do so.

Although there is no special time to initiate a four way conference, the best time in my opinion is early in the case but after the Case Information Statements have been completed. It's hard to discuss a case before information has been shared. If you at least have a CIS to work off of, the lawyers can go through the issues listed on the CIS.

I prefer to start off with the easy issues and work my way down to the more difficult ones. What will we do with the house? Is there an agreement on custody? Will we value the pensions, QDRO them, or just waive them? What about the cars? Discovering the uncontested issues and then moving past them one by one builds up momentum that can carry forward to the more difficult issues such as alimony. If both sides agree to the income figures to be used for each party, alimony shouldn't be that complicated. However, if alimony is going to be a very sticky issue, then maybe we break and come back to it another day.

If any issues remain, the lawyers can agree to focus discovery on only certain issues. If it is a one-issue case, you may even be able to grab another lawyer for a few minutes during the Case Management Conference for an impromptu ESP. You could also run that one issue by the judge. The insight given there could help settle the case very early on.

If the four way conference starts going bad, the best thing to do is leave. Almost all have gone well for me, but I did have one go bad because the client wanted to take that time to get into a fight with the other lawyer who was particularly difficult to deal with. Now I am as aggressive as it gets, but there is a big difference between being aggressive and being an a-hole. An aggressive lawyer knows when to fight and when to walk away. This client wanted me to fight even though there was no reason to. The appropriate response was to walk way. He was so upset that this other lawyer walked all over me that he fired me for someone else which is rather rare in my office. Years later, I came to find out that a rather uncomplicated case went on much longer than it should have--probably because the client wanted his lawyer to be a-hole too. Even after the divorce, the client is now representing himself as post-judgment motions have been filed, most of which are probably unnecessary. The lesson here is don't be this client. It takes a bigger person to walk away from your spouse's a-hole lawyer and regroup to discuss the strategy moving forward than to sit there, fight it out and waste time.

Chapter 13

Early Settlement Panel

Early Settlement Panel or ESP (otherwise known as Mandatory Early Settlement Panel or MESP in some counties) is your first opportunity to sit down with a lawyer appointed by the court in an attempt to settle your case. While the word panel is used to indicate that there is more than one lawyer, in some counties you only meet with one lawyer.

This lawyer is usually a lawyer who regularly practices in that county and is experienced in family law. In my opinion, the actual competence of this lawyer can vary greatly. While the practice does vary somewhat from county to county, the basic premise is that both sides will submit a position statement addressing the issues in the case for the panel's review. The panel will then issue a decision that is non-binding and non-evidential. The purpose is to hear what a neutral party thinks about your case so that you can re-evaluate your position and move towards settlement.

I should mention now that in general I am not a big fan of ESP. I sometimes joke that ESP is a several hour process to select an economic mediator (which is usually the next step in the case). Don't get me wrong, I try to keep an open mind. But in my experience practicing all around New Jersey, the ESP is is rarely helpful to me. I'll explain why in a minute. However, since it is essentially mandatory, I try to make the best out of it.

The position statement is one of the most important documents in the case. Some courts will actually give you a short fill-in-the-blank form to fill out. Regardless, most lawyers don't submit lengthy ESP statements. I like to submit a trial-memo style brief along with every relevant attachment. This sometimes results in a very lengthy statement. Very rarely will the panel want to even start to go through all of this. However, I still find it useful because all of the facts and law that support my position are thrown on the table subject to criticism. If my position is attacked, I can quickly cite to either the law on my side or take out the exhibit that supports the position.

This is where I find ESP most helpful. If it is pointed out that I am missing some facts, you can be sure that I will have them attached to the next version of this ESP statement, which will be used at economic mediation or trial. If someone cites to law that is contrary to my position, I will do the appropriate research and work that case into my statement one way or another, although I will often distinguish it from the facts of my case. Thus, while ESP may not help me settle the case right then and there, it could help me strengthen my client's case moving forward.

Besides not actually reading my statement, there are a number of other reasons why I am not a fan of ESP. Some panelists come up with the worst recommendations ever. This only makes the case more difficult to settle because now one side has heard an extreme position not grounded in reality. If there are two panelists, they may have two different opinions, which only further confuses the situation. Sometimes they only deal with one or two issues and leave the rest hanging. Some panelists just pull recommendations out of nowhere without any analysis to support them. In one case, the recommendation on an issue went against my client even though the law supported it. When I asked why they came up with a position that is clearly against the law, the reply was that it sounds like I have a good argument at trial. Uh what?! Aren't we here to avoid trial?

Don't get me wrong, I have met some amazing panelists that went beyond the call of duty to help me with my case. Some of the best lawyers in the state give up their valuable time to help out the court. Think about it, they voluntarily spend about four hours in court without getting paid. Thus, you would think that some would be more into it. I think some feel like it's their duty to serve but don't have any heart in it. Whatever the reason, it is unlikely to change anytime soon.

Your day at ESP will first start in the court room where the judge will call the calendar. He or she will then give a speech about ESP and why you should keep an open mind going into it. At some point, your case will get called to the panel. Most panels will want to speak with the lawyers first. The case will then be discussed and after both sides have had their say, the lawyers will be asked to leave as the panelists discuss the case amongst themselves. Everyone will then be brought in and the panelists will give their recommendation. The lawyers can then discuss the case with their clients and each other to see if the case is settled. If not, the court will set them up for economic mediation, although some counties will schedule the case right for trial.

Some panelists will want everyone in at the same time. I'm not always a fan of this because the lawyers lose the ability to talk more freely. Yes, we are talking about you in there and probably not saying nice things. It's nothing personal though. Sometimes it's all theater; other times it's the truth. Whatever the case is, your lawyer should have your best interest in mind so you shouldn't take offense to it.

There is no point in arguing with the panel. In the end, their recommendations mean nothing and are sometimes not supported by the facts and the law. While I will sometimes ask some questions such as my earlier example, other times I will just walk away and regroup. I have rarely seen a panel change its recommendation no matter how ridiculous it is. I have seen some clients get upset with me because I didn't argue with the panel. Of course, they didn't see me pitch their case when they weren't in there, they just saw their recommendation. No matter how much I explain that there was no point in fighting with them, the client was still upset. This client had a very hard time taking her emotions out of the case and as a result, everything I said just went in one ear and out the other. Remember that only the judge matters and having your lawyer put on a show just to make you happy will make both you and your lawyer look like fools.

Chapter 14

Economic Mediation

If you do not settle your case at ESP, your next step is likely economic mediation. However, there are a small number of counties that will force you to go right to trial. Economic mediation is the same basic principle as ESP. However, you are only meeting with one lawyer at his or her office. Instead of having to deal with several cases, that lawyer is focused solely on you. Through the court's economic mediation program, you will get two free hours of the mediator's time. The first hour is almost always spent on reviewing the case. The second hour is the first hour that you are meeting with him or her.

If your case has to go to economic mediation, you will be there for more than an hour. Thus, expect to pay this mediator's hourly rate. In most cases, this will be split equally between the parties. Keep in mind that in those counties where economic mediation is not offered, there is no reason why you cannot still go to one of these mediators. They may or may not give you the first two hours free. Maybe you can negotiate to get a one hour review of the case done for free.

Every mediator has her own way of doing things, but I have found that forceful mediators who separate the parties usually achieve the best results. In a sense, the mediator will work both sides. Some advice will be given to one side and some will be given to the other. Both lawyers are also free to discuss various issues, fears, concerns, strategy, etc. without fear that the other side will hear. An experienced lawyer knows that there is some theater going on here but rolls with it anyway.

I understand that mediators don't want to be arbitrators. It would be nice to live in a world where the mediator can get us in a room to come to a mutual understanding. That actually works sometimes. However, if we are talking about economic mediation post-ESP, that means that there is some serious dysfunction going on. As a result, a wishy-washy mediator who just throws out scenarios without being forceful is often a waste of time.

One of my favorite mediators with the best success rate I know often follows the same approach. He thoroughly reviews all documents and sketches out a possible settlement. He then separates both parties and gets a feel for their position and their personalities. He then talks to each party and the clients and tells it like it is. He comes up with practical solutions and gets right down to the point. He is forceful but at the same time, he is not trying to force anything on anyone. Instead, he is speaking from his years of experience as a divorce lawyer and a mediator. I cannot think of a time where he hasn't helped me settle a case.

Compare that to another mediator who, while a nice guy, just throws out possibilities and says we could do this, maybe we could do this, I don't know. Really? A mediator should never say I don't know. He or she should take charge of the situation and bring everyone back down to reality. Chances are, neither side has a perfect case, and the mediator needs to show the liabilities both sides face without offending them. This other mediator has not been that successful in helping me settle my cases but for some reason my adversaries choose him. Even if he does settle the case, it takes longer, which means more money the client has to spend.

Keep in mind that the mediator doesn't even have to be a lawyer. I know some really good accountants that are mediators. I have used two different accounts with great success. They have different styles, but the first one I used did a great job crunching the numbers. She also separated us and went back and forth between our rooms. She was forceful but fair. As a result, she got the job done. While the other one wasn't as forceful, she was really good about breaking everything down for us and while she is kind, she is also practical. As a result, she settles a lot of her cases as well.

Regardless of who you go with, the end goal is the same: a

settled case. If you do settle your case at mediation, you should insist on the mediator drafting up a "memorandum of understanding." This will have all of the terms that you have agreed to in clear language and signed by both parties. This way, there is no dispute as to who agreed to what. There is no need to threaten to call the mediator into court. I have seen so many cases where one party has buyer's remorse after a settlement. With a memorandum of understanding, it will be very difficult for them to back out of the settlement. Likewise, there may some items that were not discussed but have not popped up.

For example, I had a case where we thought we had settled all of the issues but the other lawyer contacted me a few days later to indicate that there were items that were not discussed and that my client should have to pay for. Luckily, I insisted on certain language in the memorandum of understanding. The exact bills my client would be responsible for were spelled out. "Everything else" would be paid for by the wife. The other lawyer explained that these new items were not discussed at mediation. I then reminded her that we had considered any and all other expenses contemplated or not and that her client had agreed to be responsible for anything and everything else. It's not my fault that she didn't catch that or consider how broad that language really was.

Chapter 15

Intensive Settlement Conference

If you do not settle your case at economic mediation, the court may set your case down for an Intensive Settlement Conference or ISC. Some courts may call this a pre-trial conference while other courts may hold something similar without actually calling it anything at all.

One version of ISC is where the court orders everyone in at 9am and does not allow anyone to leave until either the case settles or the court closes. Sitting in court all day while the bill keeps running up forces many people to throw in the towel at some point. A good judge will meet with the lawyers and give some guidance. However, some judges are afraid to be seen as pre-judging a case.

A better version of ISC is similar to ESP. Again, you are going to court to meet with a lawyer that is volunteering his or her time. However, instead of dealing with two lawyers, you are just dealing with one. Furthermore, your case may be the only case that this lawyer has. As a result, you have this person's undivided attention without the pressure to hurry through. This has proved to be very successful in counties where it is utilized.

Regardless of the exact process that is utilized, your lawyer should have an ISC memo or draft of a trial memo with him or her. This is the same document that has been drafted since ESP, but it has been refined as the case has evolved. Positions have been examined, modified, further supported and further researched. As the case advances, the ISC memo should become stronger with all of the feedback that is given.

Besides having a good ISC memo, you need to work out a plan of attack with your lawyer. What are you looking for? What are you willing to concede? If you can't settle the whole case, can you narrow down the issues to make the trial cheaper and easier? These are things you have to discuss with your lawyer. While I would avoid drawing a line in the sand, I recommend having an idea as to what you are willing to accept and what you will take to trial.

Other than child custody, every other issue in the case can be broken down to a dollar figure. Your settlement position can then be quantified to a specific figure, as can the other side's position. This will allow you to see how far apart you really are. You must factor in the cost of a trial to help evaluate your current position and what your drop dead position is. For example, if you are $40,000 apart and trial will cost you at least $30,000, do you really want to spend $30,000 to hopefully net $10,000? Of course, that is your best case scenario. You can spend $30,000 to get $20,000, at which point you are now at a $10,000 loss. The best lawyer will tell you that money is money; it doesn't matter where it goes.

Hopefully your case has been settled.

Chapter 16

The Property Settlement Agreement

Once you have an agreement on all of the issues between the two of you, it is time to put everything in writing. This document is called a Property Settlement Agreement (PSA) or Matrimonial Settlement Agreement (MSA), or sometimes even other names. The bottom line is that this document is going to be one of the most important documents in your life and as such, it should be gone over with a fine tooth comb over and over again.

The reason why it is so important is that this will come to rule your post-divorce life and that of your spouse. It will control how property is divided, who has to pay what, who has to do what with the children, etc. Keep in mind that this document isn't intended to bind you and your spouse to the same decisions forever. You two can agree to modify the PSA at any time. Instead, this document is for when you don't agree. You need to enforce your rights, and this is the document that explains what your rights are.

The best way to look at the PSA is to envision the worst case scenario. Picture yourself back in court for every single issue. It's a nightmare, of course, but you need to think about it. Ask yourself and then ask your lawyer, what will happen if your spouse doesn't.... or what will happen if we try to do this thing contemplated in our PSA but it doesn't work out. Everything needs to be spelled out.

Let's look at a common example that I see in my office. A PSA may say something like: "The parties agree that the house will be listed for sale with a mutually agreed real estate agent and that the proceeds will be split equally." Instead of a quick sale, the house lingers on the market with no offers and the listing agreement expires. Now what? Who will pay for the upkeep of the house moving forward? What if you can't agree on the next realtor? What if you want a price reduction and your spouse doesn't? What if you moved out and the spouse damaged the house? What if something else damaged the house and insurance won't cover it? What if the roof needs to be replaced all of a sudden?

If your PSA is silent on these issues, you will have to probably rehire a lawyer, file a motion with the court and then leave it up to the judge as to who should do what. You could get stuck with half or all of these expenses. The house could continue to linger on the market or you could spend thousands just to force your spouse to agree to lower the price.

Of course, all of this could have been avoided in the first place if your PSA contemplated it. Again, I realize you want to keep a positive outlook on your future divorce life, but if you don't spell every little thing out with every possible contingency planned for, you are leaving yourself open to huge problems down the road.

Once the PSA is ironed out, the court is then notified that you have a settled case so that an uncontested hearing date can be scheduled.

Chapter 17

The Uncontested Hearing

When a divorce case is settled, we say that we have "an uncontested." At some of your earlier court appearances you may have witnessed the judge "put through" several uncontested cases. Your case should really be no different. You normally don't have to prepare for anything. You should be able to just show up and have your lawyer do the rest for you. Of course, ask him or her first just to be sure.

When your case is called, your lawyer will ask you a number of questions to make sure you: 1) understand the agreement and are free from substances that would make you not understand it; 2) are entering into it voluntarily; 3) do not have any side agreements and that this is the complete agreement between the two of you; and 4) you will abide by the agreement. The whole process shouldn't take more than a few minutes.

Your lawyer will next go through the cause of action with you. These questions generally focus on where you live, where you have lived, the children you have, when you were married, when you filed for divorce, and that irreconcilable differences arose and that you want to get divorced.

Your spouse should be asked all the same questions. In some cases, your spouse may not show up. S/he could have agreed to sign everything already and thus everyone may feel that there is no reason for him/her to come to court. I would talk to your lawyer about this as he or she may want your spouse "on the record" so that s/he can be asked all of the same questions. Otherwise, s/he may have a better chance to vacate the agreement at some point in the future.

After the judge is finished with you, your lawyer will go get a gold sealed copy of the judgment of divorce. This is the official document that divorces you; the property settlement agreement is the document that governs all of the issues between the two of you. While separate documents in a technical sense, these documents are combined to dissolve the marriage between you. Thus, they are very important and should be kept in a safe place. While you can always obtain more copies if you need them, it's better to have them at the ready. You never know when you will need them.

Chapter 18

Trial

This is it. All else has failed. Your case is one of the very few that is headed towards trial. In order to succeed at trial, you have to determine why you are heading there. Where are the problems in your case? What facts are in dispute? What law is in dispute? Why can't you come up with a settlement? These questions should form the starting point for your trial strategy, and your lawyer should be able to answer all of these questions and more.

There is little you can really do except make sure that your lawyer is doing everything s/he should be doing. Some lawyers assume that the case will settle before trial and as a result, they do little to no trial prep. This decision must be part of a strategy and not simply a hope and a prayer. For example, I once had a case that I just knew was never going to trial. Thus, I didn't start any trial prep but the other side did. In fact, they spent hours on trial prep. As a result, we got to court and the fatigue and money spent preparing for trial helped us with the case. Again, this wasn't the lazy way out, but it was a specific strategy that was a little risky but worth the gamble.

As I have previously indicated, trial prep pretty much started at the beginning of the case. At this point, your lawyer should have a well-defined trial memo that the court may or may not want submitted. Discovery should be complete, and a full trial book (i.e. trial binder) should be completed. The trial book will help your lawyer keep the case organized.

You will need to understand the procedure of the trial along with the strategy to make sure that your lawyer is doing his or her job. Who will go first, in what order will the case be presented, are all exhibits in order, how will you testify and are you ready for cross examination? All of these questions must be answered to your satisfaction well before trial.

Who starts the trial and how is very important. This entire beginning should be scripted out. You don't want to be surprised by anyone at trial, let alone your own lawyer. Some lawyers don't like writing everything out, but I have found that to be very effective for my style. It also makes it easier for clients as I can almost script out their testimony. Of course, care should be taken to understand and not memorize your testimony. If you attempt to memorize your testimony but don't really understand it, your nervousness at trial could cause you to forget. I've seen it too many times. You need to understand the basic concepts and why you will say what. As a result, you don't have to worry about remembering the exact answer.

You also need to make sure your lawyer has all the exhibits. When they are finished being prepped for trial, be sure to examine them. Make sure they are complete and accurate copies. Make sure there is no writing on them that you wouldn't want anyone else to see. If you don't understand why something is being introduced or omitted, ask.

When it comes to exhibits, you also have to understand some basic rules of evidence to know how and why some exhibits will be introduced. First you have to understand the difference between marking evidence and moving evidence. Marking evidence is just for identification. When certain rules are followed, that document can be moved into evidence if the court permits same.

For example, a financial document such as a credit card statement may be entered into evidence to prove how much debt there is for this one account. The statement is a business record and proves a relevant fact so thus it should be admitted without a problem. However, a police report may be just marked for identification and not moved into evidence. The report itself is hearsay. Nonetheless, it can still be used at trial to refresh a witness' recollection. Say a witness forgets what he or she said to the police. By marking the report and showing it to him or her, the witness may now recall making those statements indicated in the

79

report. The report has served its purpose and probably won't be admitted into evidence.

Those are just basic examples, but the point is that different pieces of evidence serve different purposes. While you don't need to understand all the complex rules involving every piece of evidence, you should have a basic idea of how the whole puzzle fits together.

Also keep in mind that some items of evidence may never be used. Let's use our police report example again. Say the witness did remember exactly what he or she said to the police. Confronting the witness with the report would be pointless. Likewise, other items may be held at the ready if the other side attacks you on a certain issue. If they never do, none of these items are needed.

Most people are nervous on the witness stand, and it is amazing how many clients and witnesses have forgotten the most basic pieces of information because of this. For really big trials, you will want to consider having at least a partial mock trial. This is really high level stuff and most people don't have the money for it. However, in those cases where money isn't a problem, it should be strongly encouraged.

There is no real one way a mock trial should be handled, but one of the best ways is to actually hire someone to play judge and someone else to play the other side. It's difficult if not impossible for your own lawyer to effectively cross examine you.

Let's face it, you don't fear her because you know her very well (especially at this point!). An outsider that comes in to tear you up is the best way to simulate the real thing.

Because your lawyer is biased, it might be difficult for him or her to really judge how you held up at trial. As a result, you will want someone else to sit in to evaluate and critique your testimony. While it shouldn't be your only choice, choosing a retired judge may be the closest thing to a real world experience.

Once the mock trial is over, it is time to debrief. What does everyone think of your performance? What should be changed? What should be added, dropped, etc. Where are the holes in the case and how can they be patched? Are you going to fold under the pressure of cross examination? As a result of all of this, do you reconsider your settlement position?

After all the prep work and review, it's finally time to get down to trial. You show up to court and your lawyer has a metric ton of documents in tow. You are ready for a long, grueling day of battle, right? Wrong! There is at least some chance that you will sit there all day and never utter one word of testimony and yet, still get to pay your lawyer to sit there and play with his or her phone and roam the halls chatting with colleagues.

Unlike a jury trial where the entire thing has to be completed in order, a bench trial does not have to proceed in a timely fashion. Trial time is very sparse and a 20 hour trial can easily take months to complete. That's because a judge's notes aren't going anywhere. He or she can take as little or as much as s/he desires and/or his/her schedule permits. No one, and that includes the judge, ever really knows how much time will be available.

As I have emphasized throughout this book, family law is chaotic for everyone. The judge could have five trials scheduled and four of them could settle and as a result, you are up. Or all five can move forward and you are number five so you will wait a while. The judge could have an empty calendar one day and then a few days later, that calendar is filled with domestic violence trials, emergency motions, and other things that just seem to pop up.

Regardless of how much of the trial gets completed, you will likely have to come back another day. However, the next available trial day could be weeks away. As a result, this trial may take months to complete. There is no way your lawyer can remember everything so he or she will have to constantly prep the case as time goes on. In addition, issues always seem to come up during a divorce, so expect letters and calls back and forth to discuss these issues with the other side.

When you add it all up, a trial is a very expensive endeavor. In addition to the financial issues, it takes a toll on you emotionally. Thus, it is no wonder why only the smallest percentage of divorce cases go to trial and why not all of them actually see the case through to completion. Thus, before you jump at the chance to take the case to trial, keep all of this in mind so that you can make an informed choice.

Chapter 19

Post Judgment

No matter how well you get along with your ex or how good your PSA is worded, there is a good chance that you will be back in court at some point on a motion. This is referred to as post-judgment as it is after the judgment of divorce. In order to get back into court, you have to file a motion, which is a formal request of the court to do something.

Whether it's a post-judgment motion or some other type of motion, there are formal requirements that you must follow or else your motion will get denied regardless of the merits of your case. Thus, I highly discourage filing a motion by yourself. Have some people filed pro se motions and been successful? Of course! But countless others have been beaten down over and over again.

Don't think that you can wing it without a lawyer first and if you fail, then hire a lawyer for a do-over. It doesn't work like that.

You are held to the same standard as a lawyer, and you cannot keep filing the same motion over and over again until you get the right result. Even if a lawyer can help you, it will likely be more expensive than if you would have just hired a lawyer in the first place.

The basic motion process in New Jersey is as follows: one party files a motion and serves the other party. The other party then either files a response or a cross-motion. A response only addresses the issues raised in the motion. A cross-motion addresses those issues but also brings up new issues that this party wants addressed. In either case, the initial moving party files a reply and gets the last word. Thus, your lawyer may advise you to file your motion first if you think the other side will be filing a motion.

Almost all motions are heard on Fridays. However, there is no guarantee that your motion will be heard by the judge in open court. This is called oral argument. While you can indicate in your moving papers whether or not you want oral argument, it doesn't mean that the court will honor your request. If the court does not allow oral argument, the judge will mail out a decision.

If you go to oral argument with a lawyer, understand that your lawyer is not there to put on a show for you. Instead, your lawyer is there to create a record. The purpose behind making a record is to be able to file an appeal. Most of the time, the judge has already made up his or her mind. In fact, some judges issue "tentative decisions" before oral argument, especially when two lawyers are involved. This shows everyone what the judge is thinking and unless you can point out that the court missed something big, that is going to be the decision. For this reason, many tentative decisions are accepted by both sides.

Whatever the procedure, the court will issue an order. This order, no matter what it says, is a very important document and should be kept with your PSA. When filing future motions with the court, your lawyer will likely want your PSA along with any and all court orders.

Don't try to use motions as a way to harass the other side, and don't allow the other side to harass you. If the court finds that either side is using motion practice to harass the other or is otherwise filing a motion that is frivolous, the court can force the offending party to pay the other side's counsel fees. As I often tell my clients, we can ask for them but don't expect to get them. Post-judgment motion counsel fees are the exception and not the norm.

Hopefully you can stay out of court as much as possible. Unfortunately, some people are in court every few months. They spend years fighting each other and spending thousands on lawyers, often switching one for another. It's a sad life and everyone in court knows who these people are. If you have a good lawyer from the start, you can avoid being in that position. I know because I cannot think of a client that I represented during a divorce that had serious post-judgment problems like this.

Chapter 20

The Appeal Process

I really hope that this chapter is for entertainment only and that you don't even have to consider an appeal. In order to appeal your divorce case, you will have to go to trial and lose. As if that wasn't expensive enough, an appeal can be even more expensive. As a result, an appeal of a divorce trial is very rare. More common are appeals of divorce motions. That is why I am handling this topic after post-judgment motions since the process is basically the same for either a trial or a motion.

An appeal is a review of the trial judge. It is not a do-over. An appeal is filed with the Appellate Division, where the case will be heard by two or three judges who you will probably never even see since most appeals are done on the papers. The appeal process follows very strict procedural rules that trip up many lawyers so it is a really bad move to even think about trying this out by yourself.

Please also keep in mind that there are important deadlines that you must meet or you will lose your right to appeal. Be sure to check with your lawyer about these deadlines.

The appeal process starts with the filing of a notice of appeal and other documents. Obviously, the purpose of this document is to provide everyone with notice that you are filing an appeal. If anything was done on the record—such as testimony, oral argument or an oral decision—a transcript must be ordered. Once the transcript is received, a briefing schedule is set. Again, there are very strict requirements for the brief so please make sure you understand them.

The brief will contain, among other things, a statement of facts, procedural history and legal argument. The legal argument will focus on the standard of review, which is the standard by which the Appellate Division will review the trial court's decision. Most family court decisions are given wide discretion that the Appellate Division will often defer to. As a result, the burden to overturn a family court decision is often very high.

The easiest way to overturn a family court decision is to attack it on procedural grounds. That is, you will want to argue that the family court should have granted oral argument, discovery, a plenary hearing, etc, and did not for whatever reason. Keep in mind however that if you are successful, all you really win is the opportunity to go back in front of a family court judge. Unfortunately, you may wind up back in front of the same judge, who may not be happy to see you back in his courtroom. That is why you should request that the case be remanded to a different judge in your brief. If this request is denied, you can ask the family court judge to recuse himself/herself.

Thus, if you are not aiming for a complete reversal of the trial court's decision, you must factor in the cost of the appeal plus the remand. However, since the appeal process could take a year or more, you will have time to financially prepare for the remand if you are successful.

Chapter 21

DCPP Cases

The Division of Child Protection and Permanency, formerly known as DYFS (Division of Youth and Family Services), is the agency in New Jersey that protects children from abuse and neglect. Some divorces can include DCPP involvement in several ways including but not limited to an investigation, informal involvement in the divorce case, a separate DCPP case, an appeal of a substantiation to the Office of Administrative Law, or some combination thereof. I wrote an entire book on this subject called 'Fight back against DCPP'. Thus, I will just focus on an overview of how DCPP can impact your divorce case.

Some parents call DCPP on each other before or during a divorce case. As a result, an investigation may be launched. During this time, one or more case workers will visit the children, both p9arents and others to see if the allegations are true and if so, what should be done. Most people don't realize that DCPP is not limited to the four corners of the initial referral. Thus, if they receive a complaint about excessive corporal punishment and they quickly determine that it was false, it doesn't mean that they will go away. The investigation can go in any direction if the caseworkers see that a child may be at risk of abuse or neglect.

One of the most common areas of concern, especially in a divorce case, is substance abuse. These allegations typically come from the other parent, but they can come from any source. These allegations can be difficult to disprove as most people have been intoxicated at one point or another. Furthermore, many people smoke marijuana or have used some other drug. While marijuana tolerance and legalization is gaining steam, DCPP still views this as a serious offense. Likewise, while alcohol is legal, any use around children will raise red flags with DCPP.

If DCPP is investigating you in any way at any time, you should have a lawyer handle the entire case. Keep in mind that your divorce lawyer may not be the right lawyer to handle the case. Chances are, he or she may have no idea what to do. This is because there are a very small number of lawyers that regularly handle DCPP matters.

The goal of your lawyer is to keep the case out of court. Unfortunately, even if DCPP does not bring you to court, they can still become involved in your divorce case. Again, this is where you need competent counsel or even two lawyers; one to handle the divorce aspect of the case and one to handle the DCPP issues. The problem with this set up is that you are not afforded the same level of due process as you would be if DCPP filed a formal case against you. Your right to confront the witnesses and evidence against you may be severely limited. As a result, your lawyer should be fighting to get at least some if not all of these safeguards put in place. Getting DCPP out of your divorce case should be priority number one.

If DCPP does file a formal case against you, the custody and parenting time issues will likely be handled in that case unless and until that case is closed. Thus, the divorce case may solely focus on economic issues. If those issues are settled, the divorce case may then be put on hold until the DCPP case is resolved. The same lawyer can represent you in both cases but again, you need to make sure that the lawyer is fully equipped to do so.

Chapter 22

Domestic Violence

Some divorce cases actually start with three cases at the same time: the divorce, a restraining order, and accompanying criminal charges. However, not every restraining order comes with criminal charges, so it could just be two cases. Other times, a restraining order comes after the start of the case. Whatever the combination or timing, domestic violence allegations can have a huge impact on the divorce case.

If a temporary restraining order (TRO) is even filed, one party will be forced to leave the house. As a result, that parent's parenting time will be severely impacted if not eliminated all together. Thus, even if the TRO is eventually dismissed either voluntarily or after a trial, the impact on the divorce case can be long lasting.

Because the impact of a TRO with or without a divorce case

is so serious, the trial is usually scheduled usually within 10 days. This is again when you want to make sure that you have the right lawyer by your side. Most lawyers don't do a ton of trials. Even those that do are used to having months if not a year or more to prepare for them. During this time, a discovery period is conducted, which makes almost the entire trial a scripted affair. There are hardly any surprises.

On the other hand, a Final Restraining Order (FRO) trial is the complete opposite. Your lawyer has no idea what the other side will do or say. What exhibits will they use? What witnesses will they call? It's almost always a complete surprise. Your lawyer has to be able to wing it when all of his training and experience has taught him otherwise. You don't want to be your lawyer's guinea pig!

While the law says that TROs cannot be settled, the truth is that many of them involving a divorce case are. While the TRO itself is dismissed, a consent order is drawn up under the divorce docket number. This consent order is almost always called "Civil Restraints." While it doesn't carry the same safeguards that an FRO does, it can still provide a measure of protection for the alleged victim while allowing the defendant to escape some of the harsh penalties of the FRO. Both sides should strongly consider this alternative when faced with any restraining order trial, but especially when a divorce is involved.

If an FRO is entered against the defendant, it is final, which means that it is forever. Unlike most other states, there is no expiration date. It can only be dismissed by a court or if the victim drops it. An appeal should be strongly considered as well. Again, please note that there are important deadlines that you must meet. Be sure to discuss same with your lawyer.

If there are criminal charges with or without a restraining order, keep in mind that anything said during the divorce may be used against you in that criminal trial. Hopefully, your lawyer understands this even if s/he does not practice criminal defense. If you have one lawyer for each case, be sure that they keep in touch with each other to coordinate their defenses.

www.ingramcontent.com/pod-product-compliance
Lightning Source LLC
Chambersburg PA
CBHW051729170526
45167CB00002B/857